Digging
For Roots

✿

poems by

Kiana Davis

Caitlin!
Thank you so much for
your support! I'd love to have
you tonight!

Where there is no vision, the people perish.
~Proverbs 29:18

This book is dedicated to my family and friends.
I am thankful for all of you.
I would also like to dedicate this book to my ancestors.

When their stories didn't reach my ears,
I rebelled against my own skin
too young to realize that without their stories
I would starve.

Digging for Roots

Table of Contents

CHAPTER I
IDENTITY CRISIS

CHAPTER 2
EMBRACING BLACK WOMANHOOD

CHAPTER 3
AFTER MALCOLM

CHAPTER 4
UNREST

CHAPTER 5
EMPOWERED TO NAME LIES

Digging For Roots

Chapter 1

Identity Crisis

❧ Quest

I spent a lot
of my childhood
questioning God,
searching for brown dolls,
suppressing negative reflections,
counting absences,
calculating unspoken pain
and searching for questions
that matched answers
I created myself.

I had to wait
until young womanhood
to learn the truth behind
Black America's
tortured survival
and at 18
I began to heal
falling in love
with the very color
of my skin.

❧ Identity Crisis

At four
I began counting black dolls
for wholeness
hunting the world
outside of myself
for answers
to the deliberate invisibility.

At seven
I internalized the negative
portrayals of black women
and decided who I would
and who I would not become.
I made a decision
that I would find or create
an image for myself.

I spent my adolescence
analyzing behavior and skin
watching others
live out contrived labels
I felt like the only one
consumed by the differences
others seemed to easily sleep
while I couldn't find anyone
in my dreams brown like me
I was drowning in whiteness.

At 18
I headed down south
to Livingstone a black college,
read The Autobiography of Malcolm X,
Emerson's Self Reliance,
and began digging for roots.

Finally I was able to see myself
in books, on shelves,
on greeting cards, in artwork
and in all the places
I'd once felt absent.

ৰ A Doll Like Me

I cried for dolls
that didn't always exist on shelves
shelves that held rows and rows of dolls
for a little girl I did not know

when I got older
and stopped insisting
that all brown dolls
looked like me
stopped begging
my mother for an image
of myself to hold

she told me
she had been afraid
to come home from shopping
empty handed
afraid to bring her little girl
a pink, blue eyed, stranger

she blamed Reagan
for their absence
convinced that before him
she had no problems
finding brown dolls
 for her daughters

she told me
that sales clerks stared at her
not understanding why
she couldn't take any doll from their shelves
she said she searched stores
close to tears for me.

all I remember of those times is:
crying because I didn't understand the absence
crying because I had to leave stores empty handed
crying for a doll brown like me
crying because of pain I could not articulate.

❧ Seven's Eyes

My anger rested in things
I could not understand or control
with child eyes
I looked over the ghetto and blamed
I blamed the seemly strong
I directed my anger
toward the victims of poverty

I couldn't understand
how my community
circled pain
raging war against itself

what I did not understand
I muffled in my mind
separating the existence between us
desperate to detach air from lungs
assimilating in silence

I blamed the gun bearers,
poison pushers,
corner fillers,
not understanding
they were of me
and that poverty
left us both crippled
clawing
for more.

❧Lessons in Color

My mother never laced
my dreams in color-
she said, *"You are who you are and that's it"*

But little black girls:
were spied upon,
we were too angry,
too dirty, too loud,
had our children too young,
we were too ashy, too hungry for answers
to questions that burned ears,
busy bodies, too grown too soon.

*My mother never laced my dreams in color
I engulfed the lessons alone.*

❧Hair Story

We were little girls
who learned
to run from rain
afraid
that if our hair got wet
we'd have to sit beneath fire.

❧ Misconceptions

I thought we
were always
supposed to be on the bottom:
slaves, poor, living in ghettoized hells
idle corners held men
that could have been
strong enough to be my fathers

women were too strong
praying for love
sacrificing everything
for children and men no good
I knew a little about the writers, the doctors,
the lawyers, and the dreamers

I thought we'd always
have to wait
for the Good Times until Cosby
carried my Blackness
like a chore
until miles from home
I learned my history
and could finally
piece together what knowledge uncovered

tied to a place of longing
I built a bridge
amid my own misconceptions and the truth.

Chapter 2

Black Womanhood

ॐ Beautiful

They said
I would never be beautiful
painted me blue, black
grinning forever
big red lipped
hair standing on end

mocking God's creations

they wanted me to hate
the natural texture of my hair
to despise the color of my skin
to feel inferior under laughing eyes

but I have unearthed the beauty
behind their distorted images
wrapped hands
around hair of wool
and molded in love
stared passed masked horrors
and fell in love with dark skin
replacing their horror with beauty
and the shame with honor

they said.......

❧ Miss Sophia #1

Inspired by *The Color Purple*

Beaten down
in the middle
of her crossroads
stripped of her power to scream
demolished in the presence of her children
by a mob
who wanted her to believe
she was simply a poor,
black, crazy, women
who deserved
to be a victim of the privileged.

❧ Miss Sophia #2

After awaking
God restored
her second set of wings
and before our eyes
we watched
as she allowed herself
to accept his gifts.

ࡠ Mammy

Nestled within
her large breast
against
the true image of her strength
nurtured to silence
her inner storm
to nurse
on her brimming freedom.

❧ On my Back

I carried you
on my back
strong enough
to weep for two
and now
you want to disregard
that we were rib to rib
brown to brown

and leave me to love alone

I carried
our worlds
on my back
burnt both ends
of our love
to bear
an unimaginable
weight.

❧ Resistance

I am angry
that we were
and are still
being misrepresented
silenced into subversive submission
left to question
the importance of our visibility

I am offended because
they raped her of her homeland
to teach her to eat shit,
labeled her a jezebel, mammy,
uppity, emasculators
offended
because she was not
afforded a pedestal
but left to raise her
children in concrete jungles
filled with high rise shanties,
food stamps, bibles, and crack

breeding masochistic love

I am angry
because black little girls
are forced between knees
and straightened into
commercialized beauty
learning that naturalness
is a radical step toward
severed African roots

I am angry because
I didn't learn of my
heritage until I was 18
and had to dig up
the truth with fingernails
shaped into blades.

❧ Black Girl Lost

I have
bitten down
on my own tongue
not to succumb to characterizations
bitten down
on the best parts of myself
to be loved
pulled together
someone else's puzzle pieces
to connect
searched for myself
in images that never
resembled my own
lost.

& There is Pride in Being

There is pride in being a black woman
There is pride in being a descendant of warriors,
who possessed the strength to live
through hell and remain composed.
I am proud to be a seed of slaves.
I am a reflection of ancestors
who could have given in but held on for me.
I am the outcome of the shame.
I am the outcome of the brutality.
I am the reason for the marches.
I am the reason for the dream.
I am the reason they died to be free.
I am their prayers come true.
The manifestation
of unbreakable spirits and swollen hearts.
I am proud.

❧ American Flag

I deserve to wrap you
Red, White, and Blue around my head
and wear you like a crown for my mothers
who did without liberty and whose love
the pursuit of happiness could not ease
justice for all or the pain of their babies
growing up under God we trust
to
face
separate
and
not
equal

❧ Sarrtjie Baartman 1810

Her abundant beauty
baffled them
treated like a clown
they paraded her around
as if she were a freak of nature

ashamed of my body
until I read her story
I wish I could have
been taught her name
while growing up
a young girl
with a woman's body

my own mother's eyes
watched me for signs
of fastness
covering me up
in oversized clothes
teaching me
that the black woman's body
was an object of shame

I had the power
somehow
to tempt men to destruction.

Too Long

I've held your eyes too long
and listened too closely to your voices
cringing, embarrassed for both of us
I've studied your hair,
clothes, and actions too long
rolling my eyes when I find you
the way they've described you
I can't enjoy your presence
without first looking you over
making sure you fit
into their suppressed
image of pretense.

❧Universality

I know
that she is not
the only one
who has been
slaughtered
and that I should
grow wings

true empathy
can only come
from learning
of her sisters' sorrows

but my mothers' stories
were withheld
and I will sit
at her feet
until her stories
have been told.

❧ Thank You

Audre Lorde, Toni Morrison, Maya Angelou, Gloria Naylor, Alice
Walker, Asha Bandele, Tanarive Due, Iyanla Vanzant, Octavia Butler

Inside the books
on my crowded shelves
lives God

written by women
who channeled
their gifts and birthed worlds
I've had the pleasure to travel

words
that have stripped me
down to nakedness
and frantically I've searched
my flesh for answers

stripped my mind
until I've spoken words
that honored my knowing.

women
who have challenged me
to pry open my mouth
and speak my sounds
into existence

women
who have inspired me
to clamor under rain
and dance self-worth

women
whose wisdom have sat me down
and feed me
life's cruel beauties
sometimes their words
felt crammed down my throat
but I managed to swallow them.

I have glimpsed
genius so pure
in all of you
and each story
has given me the courage
to honor my filled cup.

৯ Judgment

I don't know who
they are listening for
and it won't be
reincarnated here

You won't find
Hemingway in
my voice
or Emily in my steps

My sound will
be more like
Tubman's and Lorde's
I want to free the caged bird
and help Solomon find his song

A little black girl
who trusted voices
into womanhood
finding her voice
after digging free
from being buried
under lies

I can relate evenly
with the words
coming out of my mouth
I don't know what
they are looking for
but my sound
will bleed freedom.

❧ Oprah

At 11
I watched her in awe
a young girl disillusioned
casting dreams
toward unclaimed shadows

she gave my hope wings
and I began to aspire again
believing in images beyond
the train tracks and poverty mindsets

she inspired me to stand taller than
I had ever imaged I could
she made me proud
to one day become a Black woman.

Chapter 3

After Malcolm

❧ Malcolm X

Stretched out on white paper
I found myself
typed out perfectly in black ink
and I have not been the same

freshman year
I read your story
and if your story was real
my knowledge
was one sided
and my side
the missing side

you taught me
to find pride in my reflection
and to hold love for the past
and so began
the burning hunger
engulfing me
I read 40 books
in three months
starved for answers-
four years later
my library was full grown.

❧ Family Affair

Million Women March 10/25/1997
Benjamin Franklin Parkway in Philadelphia

We stood together
chanting
1.5
for the number of women
1.5
that had come together
1.5
in search of change and sisterhood

I remember
standing under the pleas
of our History Makers
as they urged us to
forge a bond as sisters

I held up a mirror
above my head
examining the sea
of brown faces
proud to be a part
of dreamers dreams

There was an announcement
of a lost child
and a little boy
appeared in the crowd
crying for his mother

I marveled at the fact
that he was surrounded
by a million mothers
who reached out to him
to soothe his pain
and heal the rift
of a battered past
and neglected sisterhood

~ 1997

❧ We Sang

A sweet melody
through the cracked lips
of the wounded

gathered together
to ease the pain
of toiling

we sang

waiting for our Savior

praying to be liberated
voices on one accord
singing one song
during one time of mourning
to a merciful Father.

We sang.

~ 1996

❧ Black Bird

In flight
you remind me of Kings
warriors bronzed by the sun

blessed with the gift of flight
I watch you run
towering over air
as you leap for a shot

daydreaming
I see the indignities
of poverty wiped away
ghettos banished
our community is restored.

~ 1996

ৰ Map of Africa

I know all the names
by heart
I can tell you where
they all lay
flat
stretched out
on blue paper
I have yet to feel its sun
but I know it is real

~ 1997

❧ Freedom

Inspired by Margaret Walker's Jubilee

If you say you love me
meet me under the tree of life
come alone without shadows
when the light of day
hangs in the sky like a ball of white fire

Come when
only the sounds of evening
echo through
the souls of dead men
who were unable to reach me

Come when
all labor is done
when the Big House
is blackened with sleep

Come when
your heart is bursting
run until you are able to touch me
find my face in the luminous North Star.

Continue on
if you say you love me.

~ 1997

❧ My Black Nascent

Beneath the maples and the oaks
I feed on your journeys
and began
like a baby
to crawl to you

I learned to walk
by falling to stand
only to stand to fall
and when
I was finally able to walk
I found you
sitting next to injustice free.

Chapter 4

Unrest

❧ Scattered

They separated
us by age
and raped us
of our elders
so when the young
grew old
they would not
bite down
too hard
on hands that feed them
their own bloody flesh.

❧ It Goes Back

It goes back
to the shores
of our mother's womb
back when
we were sold
by our own hands

It goes back
to the shackles
back when
we were strapped side by side
and couldn't understand each other
enough to stand on common ground
and fight our way free

It goes back
to the lies
we were fed
each generation
eating a portion
of their bullshit

It goes back.

❧ Descendants

We live in abundance
swallowing everything whole
without healing
living from
a place of denied pleasures.

❧ Digging for Roots

We've come together
to dig up your roots,
to expose truth to the sun,
to fill our mouths with prayers,
to sing the songs left behind,
to step into your shoes
and walk under the weight,
to dance inside your shadows,
to thank you for your survival,
to kiss our elders lips
who agonized
and died for us.

❧ For You

This is for you
who paved the way
treaded over bones
crossed seas of blood
added dirges and prayers
to a sacred place
time gathered for us
under glorious trees.

❧ Unrest

Someone asked me why
I keep you alive
breathing life
into your memories
hanging your faces on walls
collecting your stories on shelves
they say
I cause your spirits unrest
and yet,
I feel compelled
to arm myself
with knowledge
once withheld
to know you all
and call you by name.

~ Give You Place

They don't want to give you
a place in their lives
they say:
"you bring bad memories
and we should move on"

while other cultures
revere their past with pride
they say let's leave our dead behind

those who toiled
would have never left us
they would have opened up
their shot gun shanties
offered whatever they had
their lasts
to help us along the way.

but now that their hard work
allows breathing easier
they disregard
hundreds of years
millions of lives
to bask in the blood
and silence the broken stories.

❧Under my Feet

I have shed tears
for our loses
and I will continue
to cry for you
until a river
forms under my feet.

❧ Burning Images

Images of their suffering
has scorched
my mind's eye
and for days
I must hold my tongue
not to scream.

They murdered innocence,
mangled black fatherhood
and tortured the
black woman to stone

My silence is often
questioned
and I can't look
anyone in the eyes
without feeling the lost
like it is fresh
and the burden is mine
alone.

Chapter 5

Empowered to Name Lies

❧ Difference

There is a difference
between our stories
an invisible line
drawn down the backs
of the oppressed.

❧ Black Like Me

Heading home
on a crowded train
my past enters
and sits across from me

He is the color
of my childhood
mud pies
familiar darkness

watching him
I remember summers
chasing butterflies, filling jelly jars with tadpoles,
black berries, clobbers, and my brother Kevin

Looking up
he sees me watching
he thinks I am flirting
but I am trying to touch a mystery.

❧ *Amadou* Diallo

Death has come before
like this
unexpected camouflage
someone's child
has been murdered before
leaving behind
broken hearts and questions
but I will
etch your name
among those murdered
I will remember your family
in prayers
I will not let you die
with 41 shots
echoing in your ears.
I hope your spirit
finds absolution
and that your death
wakes up sober souls
that have slept through this war,
Diallo.
I hope your story insights rage
They say justified– we say homicide

~ 1999

❧ Reminders

These people
will smile
in your face
and chew u
whole
without blinking.

❧ Regressing

I find myself
once again
traveling back in time
offering silent apologizes
for actions
that are not mine
but committed in brown skin
I stop myself
when this happens
ashamed that I have regressed.

❧ Without Purpose

Save not yourselves but those who are left behind

There is anger, foul
on the mouths of babes
and I watch them
daily
rapping death
onto their lives
selling their bodies
for cheap attempts for love
wild,
these children
who do not know
their ancestors
names by heart
kill over
transparent honor
with lifeless eyes
living without purpose

I have
reached out to them
wanting to feed them
the knowledge
that has saved me

but they've pulled back
full on stereotypical depictions,
cycled living,
comfortable carrying around the same dream
in long lines
I watch them
follow each other
like lambs to slaughter.

❧ Rooms

I don't know why I search
but I must look for you
count your faces
and wait for our eyes to meet
so that we can acknowledge
each other
knowing the presence between us
is greater than ourselves.

Then there are those times
when you avoid me
stare past me
as if I don't exist
we are black
but we ain't kin
and I am left
to salute our triumphs alone.

❧ Subtle Racism

It does not beat my soul
in two it does not
beat my soul in two.

৵ Strange

It is strange that you
who taught us to be monsters
would carry our masks now
fearing dark fist
afraid of violence
behind rage
you deny
you understand.

You Speak so Well

I am tired
of being on guard
feeling a sense of umbrage
as my words are devoured
with an invisible measuring stick
their attempt
to compliment is always the same
"you speak so well."

❧ Birthright

Fighting to be men
these young
murder their own skin
as a rites of passage

❧ Black Man

broken
down until
displaced rage
replaces honor
no one can pacify
being stripped
and then smiled upon
like the nakedness
does not exist
and the cold breeze
is not reality.

❧ Rosa Parks

There is so much blood
on their tongues
but today I listened
as they stopped
for Rosa Parks
a freedom fighter,
a woman warrior

I watched them
revere her courage
wishing
I could have traveled to her
I bowed my head
where I stood
believing
she could hear my thank you.

~ 2005

❧ Signals

When white boys
become angry
enough to throw blows
or to blow up the world
they are cut open
everyone wants to know
what has gone wrong
and what needs to be fixed
but angry black boys
are overlooked
left to bleed
on the hands
of their silencers
and when they explode
the world turns its head
it is common practice
that their anger
be kept behind bars

❧Brother's Eyes

Is there a right
to the anger?
a right to the rage?
I've stared
into my own
brothers eyes
and witnessed
their confused
attempts to be men.

❧ December 4th

Inspired by Shawn Carter

His story
helps me
take my seven year old self
by the hands
she is still angry
over the corners
perplexed over the fallen

she believes
that they could have been stronger
and a decision
to live beyond bars, crack sales,
and misogynist smoke screens
could have saved them

She has always wanted more than I could give

his songs
help me dissect
the twisted struggles
of growing up in jungles
facing manhood
without concrete father figures
navigating corners
to fulfill basic needs

his lyrics decode
the seeming seduction
of power and money.

he helps me understand
my older brother,
who's been imprisoned
longer than I've witnessed
his freedom

he helps me swallow
words that have only blamed
so that I can forgive
everything I have
not been able to understand
only judged.

❧ Murder of Innocence

I hate to leave out names
although the list grows daily
collecting them all
feels like standing
in the middle
of a down pour
determined to save
every rain drop-
each filled with a story
worthy of remembrance

holding them
inside my palms
brings the heaviness
of contemplative action
my grip is firm
hand slightly on top of hand
pressed fingers together
to prevent another loss

words to describe
senseless acts
allude me
and I have sat in silence
reflecting on dark hoodies, baggy jeans,
ice tea, bags of candy, loud music,

profiling, police brutality,
innocent young scholars and drive-bys casualties,
inside the wars
raging throughout America

There are no excuses
for the massacres
eroding the community
of survivors' children

I have made a firm promise
to keep their stories alive
so that I am able to explain
to the next generation
why we let so many young die.

❧ Feeding My Vision

Let the dead
bury the dead
because I'm still here waiting
holding onto hope for you
trying to make
sense of you
falling through cracks
I believe I am here
to write this way
dissecting lies
turning labels
into mirrors
and death into reawakening.

❧ I Could...

I could cry for you
but not even
the salt in my tears
can dry up your pain
or heal your wounds

with tied hands
I watch
as you live
within a reoccurring nightmare
conditioned to the belief
that we were created
to live this way.

❧ Conjuring Love

Dr. Martin Luther King Jr.

We gathered under his voice
because he had the courage
to bare our sorrows
humanizing our dark skin

He taught us
to stand for peace
without fear
to let go of shame
and fight for equality

we followed him
because he walked his dreams
and dared to fight back
against a system
that killed
to keep us out
of their
apple pie reveries

He conjured love
that moved the world
leaving our children
with a martyr
that can never be
silenced or denied.

❧ On That Day

My seven year old self
peered outside of me
smiling
she was there when I read Malcolm
and she is the mother of my libraries.

excited that the day had come
she smiled through me
and I watched her
as she slowly danced
inside the center of my heart.

and when the first daughters
walked across
the White House lawn
we closed our eyes
pretending they are us.

About the author

Kiana Davis was born and raised in
Richmond, California. She began
writing poetry at the age of 12 to
grapple with growing up in a low
income community and to help her
develop her identity as a young black
girl in America. She earned her
Bachelor's degree from Livingstone
College, one of the historical black
institutions.

For the past 10 years, she has worked
as an educator teaching at-risk youth
in Washington State.